T0119378

A Research Agenda for Assessing the Impact of Fragmented Governance on Southwestern Pennsylvania

Sally Sleeper, Henry Willis, Stephen Rattien, Adrienn Lanczos

Prepared for the Heinz Endowments

RAND INFRASTRUCTURE, SAFETY, AND ENVIRONMENT

The research described in this report was conducted for the Heinz Endowments by RAND Infrastructure, Safety, and Environment (ISE), a unit of the RAND Corporation.

Library of Congress Cataloging-in-Publication Data

Sleeper, Sally.
  A research agenda for assessing the impact of fragmented governance on southwestern Pennsylvania / Sally Sleeper, Henry Willis, Stephen Rattien, Adrienn Lanczos.
    p. cm.
  "TR-139."
  Includes bibliographical references.
  ISBN 0-8330-3639-4 (pbk.)
  1. Allegheny County (Pa.)—Politics and government. 2. Pittsburgh (Pa.)—Politics and government. 3. Local government—Pennsylvania—Case studies. 4. Municipal services—Pennsylvania—Allegheny County. 5. Municipal services—Pennsylvania—Pittsburgh. 6. Municipal powers and services beyond corporate limits—Pennsylvania—Allegheny County. I. Title.

JS451.P9A453 2004
320.9748'85—dc22
                                                                        2004010755

The RAND Corporation is a nonprofit research organization providing objective analysis and effective solutions that address the challenges facing the public and private sectors around the world. RAND's publications do not necessarily reflect the opinions of its research clients and sponsors.

RAND® is a registered trademark.

Published 2004 by the RAND Corporation
1776 Main Street, P.O. Box 2138, Santa Monica, CA 90407-2138
1200 South Hayes Street, Arlington, VA 22202-5050
201 North Craig Street, Suite 202, Pittsburgh, PA 15213-1516
RAND URL: http://www.rand.org/
To order RAND documents or to obtain additional information, contact
Distribution Services: Telephone: (310) 451-7002;
Fax: (310) 451-6915; Email: order@rand.org

Preface

In July 2003, the Program on Economic Opportunity at the Heinz Endowments asked the RAND Corporation to develop a framework to begin to explore the potential effects of fragmented local governance in Southwestern Pennsylvania and, in particular, in Allegheny County. At issue was whether the current structures for municipal, City of Pittsburgh, and county governments create inefficiencies in the cost, coverage, and quality of delivered services. Furthermore, does this fragmentation inhibit timely and comprehensive decisionmaking for public infrastructure projects and comparable private developments? This report describes the key elements that are required to address these questions.

This research was conducted within RAND Infrastructure, Safety, and Environment (ISE), a unit of the RAND Corporation. The mission of ISE is to improve the development, operation, use, and protection of society's essential man-made and natural assets; and to enhance the related social assets of safety and security of individuals in transit and in their workplaces and communities. The ISE research portfolio encompasses research and analysis on a broad range of policy areas including homeland security, criminal justice, public safety, occupational safety, the environment, energy, natural resources, climate, agriculture, economic development, transportation, information and telecommunications technologies, space exploration, and other aspects of science and technology policy.

Inquiries regarding RAND Infrastructure, Safety, and Environment may be directed to:

> Debra Knopman, Director
> 1200 S. Hayes Street
> Arlington, VA 22202-5050
> Tel: 703.413.1100, extension 5667
> Email: ise@rand.org
> http://www.rand.org/ise

Contents

Figures

Tables

Summary

The large number of municipal governments in Allegheny County is a derivative of Pennsylvania's governance structure and history. This structure provides for strong representation at the local government level. The anticipated benefit of this is a greater sense of local "ownership," encouraging local government to be responsive to constituent demands. The flipside of local representation is government fragmentation, with potential costs in the form of inefficiency and conflicting intercommunity goals.

The RAND Corporation was asked to begin to explore and create a framework for studying the effects of Pennsylvania's locally dominated governance structure on regional performance and to identify potential lessons for Allegheny County from the experiences of other regions.

Drawing from the literature, case studies, and local economic data sets, we investigated the empirical validity of two questions to understand whether they were worth pursuing in greater depth: Does multiplicity of local governance create inefficiencies in the cost, coverage, and quality of delivered services? And, does this multiplicity inhibit timely and comprehensive decisionmaking for regional economic development?

The arguments for increased regionalism are intuitively appealing yet also difficult to prove quantitatively. The historic pattern of local governance has generated frictions between suburban and urban entities, as well as racial, income, and resource imbalances among communities; inefficiencies in service provision; increased power by the private sector in shaping development patterns; and a lack of rational regional planning. On the other hand, local governance provides representation and accountability for local preferences. Finding a balance point between regional and local approaches to governance rests on knowing what the attributes of a region currently are (e.g., through performance measurement and benchmarking of services), knowing what it wants to become (e.g., through regional visioning of future development), and having an informed understanding of the likely benefits and costs of various routes of getting there.

Our preliminary analysis and literature review provide insights into the links between government structure and quality (effectiveness and efficiency) of local governance. Fragmentation can affect the cost and quality of government services, the level and perceived fairness of tax structures, and the alignment of public- and private-sector decisionmaking with regional goals.

Several models of government cooperation and coordination are available to address inadequacies in each of these areas. These models vary in their benefits, pitfalls, and level of effort required to institute and manage them, and none offers a "silver bullet" that will solve the multifaceted issues faced in this or other regions.

Recent budgetary pressures have motivated new discussions of the quality of local governance in Allegheny County and alternatives to improve it. Meaningful discussions of governance in Allegheny County need to begin by engaging municipalities in discussions about local governance and potential cooperation or consolidation options.

Careful performance assessment of the costs, utilization, and quality of municipal services will help leaders understand where Allegheny County stands, which functions are largely consolidated and which are highly fragmented, and how much citizens of the county pay in taxes. Understanding the costs and benefits to various regional interests provides the foundation to meaningfully discuss the future development of the county and to assess whether (and in what way) alternative policies will make a difference.

Even though discussions of governance have begun in Allegheny County, there are significant barriers to agreement on a model for local or regional governance. The examples presented in this preliminary report provide an overview of the important characteristics of local government and examples from other regions of achievements gained through restructuring. More definitive information, along the lines discussed in the report, can provide a foundation to move forward and, if potential benefits are apparent, to define a unified vision and set of goals for governance and economic development in Allegheny County.

Acknowledgments

We would like to thank the many members of the RAND research staff who helped us in the refinement of the ideas within. Specifically, we wish to thank participants at the RAND-Pittsburgh Research Seminar, Barry Balmat and Debra Knopman. We also greatly appreciate the comments from our reviewers, David Shlapak of the RAND Corporation and Jeffrey Hunker of Carnegie Mellon University, who provided insightful comments. We greatly appreciate the hard work and careful eyes of our support staff, Stephanie Sutton and Christina Pitcher.

Invaluable in our research process were the contributions of knowledge and insight provided during our meetings and discussions with business and community leaders. We also would like to thank Brian Kelley and the Heinz Endowments for sponsoring our research.

1. Introduction

Many observers in Southwestern Pennsylvania and Allegheny County believe that the fragmentation of regional governance among literally hundreds of entities leads to waste and inefficiency in the public sector and adversely affects the region's economic growth. To assess the legitimacy of these observations, the RAND Corporation was asked to begin to explore and create a framework for studying the effects of Pennsylvania's locally dominated governance structure on regional performance and to identify potential lessons for Allegheny County from the experiences of other regions.

We looked for evidence in literature, case studies, and local economic data sets to explore the empirical validity and explanatory value of government fragmentation. The literature on the effects of local governance on service efficiency, effectiveness, and quality and on economic development is diverse; yet, it does not demonstrate a consensus of lessons learned.

Accordingly, to begin addressing the question of whether fragmented local governance is hurting Southwestern Pennsylvania—and if so, what to do about it—we first need a research framework to help refine the question and guide our analysis. This report describes the key elements of such an approach. We do this by describing critical components for understanding the quality of governance, lessons from other communities that have experimented with different forms of local government, and alternatives that could be considered for Allegheny County. As such, the report does not present conclusions or recommendations regarding local governance in the region. It instead discusses how to undertake the work needed to reach such conclusions and recommendations.

Section 2 motivates this research by providing an overview of the potential effects of fragmented governance on local governments' delivery of services and role in regional decisionmaking. In the next section, we outline three components of local governance quality and the evidence in the literature related to these aspects. The fourth section describes models of local governance that have been adopted across the United States with attention to how the form of governance affects the components of governance quality. The final section presents observations and directions for research that can inform ongoing discussion of governance in Allegheny County. The appendix analyzes per-capita expenditures on government services in Allegheny County to provide simple insights into the performance of local governance.

2. Why Study Approaches to Local Governance?

Local governments may serve many important functions. Two sets of these functions are important determinants of the quality of life and economic performance in a region. First, government provides community services that would otherwise not be adequately available through the private sector. Many of these services provide a public good (e.g., public parks or police protection) or regulate costs of services when a natural monopoly exists locally (e.g., sewer and water treatment). Second, through taxation policies, facilities permitting, and zoning decisions, local government plays an important role in fostering a fair and competitive environment where entrepreneurship and innovation can flourish.

Responsibilities for these two sets of government functions are highly distributed in Allegheny County. Allegheny County government is largely responsible for providing public health and welfare services across the county. The 130 municipalities within Allegheny County, of which Pittsburgh is the largest, hold responsibilities for many of the other government services, including fire, police, education, sewer, and water. As discussed below, the extent of fragmentation varies widely across the range of services. For example, there are more than 200 volunteer firefighting organizations, more than 100 independent police departments, 43 school districts, and 39 water authorities in the county.

The large number of municipal governments in Allegheny County is a derivative of Pennsylvania's governance structure and history. Some have argued that this structure provides for strong representation at the local government level. The generally accepted benefit of this structure is a greater sense of local "ownership," encouraging local government to be responsive to constituent demands. The flipside of local representation is government fragmentation, with potential costs in the form of inefficiency and conflicting intercommunity goals.

In response to these perceived deficiencies, some communities have restructured local governance. Under the auspices of cooperation and consolidation, local governments have regionally concentrated service provision, permitting authorities, and tax policies to create a more unified approach to regional planning.

The arguments both for increased regionalism and for strong local governance are intuitively appealing, sometimes at odds with each other, and also difficult to prove. The major problem with strong local governance is that it may lead to fragmentation, which arises from the absence of a single government with the power to look out for the good of the region as a whole. Because of this, the struggles between suburban and urban entities result in racial, income, and resource imbalances in a region; problems in service provision; increased power by the private sector in shaping development patterns; and the lack of rational regional planning [e.g., see 4, 6, 25, 36, 56]. On the other hand, the home rule authority of local governments is important in that it provides representation closest to home and accountability for local preferences. What is the balance point, if one exists, between regional and local needs and responsibilities? We hope that our study of approaches to local governance will provide a framework for helping the county find a balance.

Allegheny County and the City of Pittsburgh are under stress. Over the past 30 years, the county and the city have lagged the nation in creation of jobs and growth of regional exports, leaving the region's manufacturing-based economy at risk [53]. The flight of young professionals from the region and an inability to attract immigrants have both contributed to population declines and an aging population [42]. Is there a relationship between regional performance and local governance?

Some local government and business leaders have suggested that fragmented local governance is responsible for the stalled economic development in the county and the city [16]. Throughout the United States, economic stagnation or decline has been more common in areas with greater government fragmentation, as illustrated in Table 2.1. As depicted in the table, there is an inverse relationship between the amount of fragmentation of a region and performance, as measured by population and job growth. Is the relationship meaningful or simply driven by factors other than government structure? It is likely that there are many factors at play. However, it is worth noting that the Pittsburgh municipal statistical area (MSA), which has the greatest number of local governments[1] per 100,000 residents, also is the weakest performing of the six most fragmented regions. Is fragmentation the only, or even major, driver? The remainder of this report lays out a research framework for better understanding whether there is a causal relationship between performance and fragmentation.

----

[1] "Local governments" include municipality, township, and county governments.

Table 2.1
Indicators of Regional Performance by Degree of Government Fragmentation
(in percentage)

Region	Population Change, 1970–2000	Job Growth, 1970–2000	Manufacturing Growth, 1970–2000	Population In-migration, 1995–2000
Six least fragmented cities	106	177	59	18
Six most fragmented cities	14	63	−20	9
Pittsburgh MSA[a]	−11	25	−54	6

SOURCE: Economic and demographic data are from the U.S. Census Bureau.

NOTES: Greater fragmentation is correlated with poor regional performance on economic and population growth metrics. Pittsburgh, which is the most fragmented of cities in the United States, lags among the six most fragmented cities. Government fragmentation is measured as the number of local governments per 100,000 residents. For this metric, the six least fragmented cities are San Diego, Los Angeles, Phoenix, Miami, San Francisco, and Tampa, in order of increasing fragmentation. The six most fragmented cities are Cleveland, Kansas City, Cincinnati, St. Louis, Minneapolis-St. Paul, and Pittsburgh, again in order of increasing fragmentation (Orfield and Katz, 2002 [59]).

[a] Pittsburgh MSA plus Armstrong, Indiana, and Greene Counties.

3. Components of Local Government Quality

There are three distinct components to assessing the impact of local governance on regional performance: (1) how and what services are provided, (2) how tax revenues are collected, and (3) how local government affects public- and private-sector location and investment decisions. The level and quality of each of these may be influenced by the structure of local governance. The means of provision—locally versus regionally or public versus private—can have an effect on the quality and cost of the services. Even when the structure of government does not affect the *amount* of taxes collected, it can impinge on perceptions of fairness about tax policies. Finally, the structure of local governance has implications for whether communities in the region work together or at cross purposes, whether citizens have a voice in government decisions, and whether local government presents barriers to entrepreneurship and economic growth.

How and What Public Services Are Provided?

Research and case studies suggest that some government services are best provided at a regional level based on (1) a need for coordination across political borders, (2) the potential for capturing economies of scale through shared labor or the use of capital facilities and equipment, (3) desires for more equitable distribution of resources, or (4) the potential to achieve win-win benefits for the entire region [e.g., see 4, 5, 29, 56, 61].

These criteria can be used to consider the current provision of many government services. Services such as water, sewer, parks, and highways may already be served by regional entities because they naturally cross municipal or county boundaries. Capital-intensive services—such as Emergency Medical Services, solid waste treatment, and public safety—may present cost-saving opportunities when expensive capital equipment can be shared across a larger population. Economic development activities generally align with regional criteria because of the need to promote, market, and grow a region. Public welfare and finance functions—such as public health, public assistance, education, and property taxing systems—are often redistributive programs designed to narrow intra-regional inequities.

The motivations for private provision of public services are similar to some of those for consolidation. A 1995 survey of privatization of municipal services in 66 of America's 100 largest cities [20] found that the most important factors in their decision to privatize specific services were to reduce costs and improve services.[2] In every service area, respondents reported that service delivery improved with privatization, by an average improvement of about 25 percent, and costs decreased between 16 percent and 20 percent. The relevance for governance is that privatization is an accepted alternative for providing (principally labor-intensive) services.[3]

Some services already are provided on a relatively more regional scale in Allegheny County, such as waste management (more than 20 solid waste management providers ranging from city authorities to private companies) and water treatment (39 water authorities or entities). Sewer services are moderately regional, with 51 sewer-related authorities in the county.

The question remains, then, does fragmentation or even "relative" consolidation affect regional performance? Should a metropolitan area have more than one provider for any of its services? If so, which ones and what are the effects on the region? There may be opportunities to further regionalize some services, but the gains in efficiency would need to be assessed relative to the effects on service quality. Balancing these factors requires measuring government performance.

The most common metric for assessing provision of government services is per-capita cost. It is frequently collected, widely published, and well accepted as a metric of government performance. Data are available from the U.S. Census Bureau for counties and large cities in the United States. State and regional organizations have also produced breakdowns of these data for smaller jurisdictions.[4] These cost data provide a useful benchmark for identifying whether local government is spending at an appropriate level for a particular function. However, answers to this question are only complete if metrics of service quality are also included, which is seldom the case.

----

[2] Other possible survey responses for reasons to privatize included reducing the number of public employees, limiting legal liability, raising revenue, reducing union influence, and augmenting employee skills. Pittsburgh, in particular, may be sensitive to issues of unionization, which creates barriers to privatizing some services.

[3] Privatization proponents argue that the biggest gains come from off-loading labor-intensive, rather than capital-intensive, services. Opponents maintain that the savings, then, are due to private-sector employment practices of lower salaries and benefits and, indeed, of hiring part-time workers with no benefits, placing a strain on other community services.

[4] For example, the Pennsylvania Department of Community and Economic Development publishes expenditure data for all municipalities in Pennsylvania at its web site—www.inventpa.com.

Cost of government services data do not indicate how much or what kinds of services are provided. The Appendix provides an analysis of the costs of government services across municipalities in Allegheny County. The analysis demonstrates that there is significant variability in costs for services across the municipalities in Allegheny County. The reasons for the variation are not immediately apparent, and they could reflect opportunities to capture economies of scale, local preferences for a higher level of service, or simply wasteful spending.

Metrics and measurement techniques to show the quality of government services delivered are well developed.[5] However, few data exist nationally as benchmarks of service quality, and even fewer have been collected and organized to document the level, resource utilization, and quality of government services in Allegheny County.

How Are Tax Revenues Collected?

Just as cost and quality are both important for government services, citizens also are acutely aware of their tax payments to government. The total tax burden imposed on citizens and companies can affect decisions about where people live and companies locate [e.g., see 35].

Changes to the structure of local governance do not ensure simpler tax systems or lower taxes [56, 83]. The consolidation of the urban core of Indianapolis with suburban areas inside Marion County offered the potential for financing the public costs of the redevelopment plan across a diverse and generally more affluent tax base than the core city itself [69, 83]. However, restructuring of tax rates was complicated by the number of taxing authorities and differences in tax rates within the region. City tax rates are higher than those in other parts of the county because the suburban tax base does not cover the consolidated public safety, education, and public assistance services. Prior to consolidation, the many overlapping and duplicative units of government resulted in taxpayers facing up to 10–16 taxing units. Post-consolidation, it is not clear that the situation has improved, in part because there has not been a simplification of the tax code. Taxes have increased since consolidation, and there has been a proliferation of taxing units. Satisfaction with the consolidation appears to be mixed. While the consolidation did not eliminate smaller urban service-delivery boundaries that

---

[5] For a discussion of these techniques see Harry P. Hatry, Louis H. Blair, Donald M. Fisk, John M. Greiner, John R. Hall, Jr., and Philip S. Shaenman, *How Effective Are Your Government Services?* Second Edition, Washington, DC: Urban Institute, 2001.

were important to different communities, the partial consolidation of the tax structure and the emphasis on service distribution on a small scale has led to some fiscal inequities in service provision, which the region currently is working to redress [69].

As a second example, all services and levels of government in Lexington, KY, were consolidated [83]. All services are now provided countywide, including police, fire, schools, street maintenance, parks and recreation, and centralized administration. There has been a decrease in property taxes every year since 1974 (the City of Lexington and Fayette County were consolidated in 1972). However, this does not tell the entire story—the countywide payroll tax rate increased from 2 percent to 2.5 percent, and several services are financed with new user fees, including sewer, landfill, and refuse collection.

Analyses by the Pennsylvania Economy League and others [26, 63] provide an overview of taxation in Allegheny County that offers two important insights, which contrast sharply with public opinion. First, a comparison of the overall tax burden faced by citizens in Allegheny County as compared with that in other regions nationally suggests that the region does not face unusually high tax burdens. Despite this finding, residents perceive their tax burden to be too high relative to the government functions and services provided. Second, while demographic shifts and flight of residents out of the City of Pittsburgh and into surrounding municipalities has reduced the city's tax base, jobs within the city have not seen a similar decline, because residents of surrounding communities continue to be employed in the city. Accordingly, city and suburban residents ask whether a change in governance would merely redistribute or increase taxes without meaningful changes in service quality [e.g., 61, 70].

Changes in government structure may not affect the level of tax revenues. However, such changes can influence the way revenues are generated and shared and, thus, how citizens perceive the fairness of tax policies [36].[6] Models of revenue sharing—such as source-based income taxes, redistribution of property taxes, and school taxes—can contribute to balancing payments and benefits [35, 56]. Measuring the cost, quality, and utilization of government services and communicating the benefits to residents are critical components of

----

[6] Behavioral economics research shows that people not only compare their situation to the way it was in the past, they also frequently and automatically compare what they get (or lose) in a situation to what they think is *fair*. Fairness depends not only on the outcomes that people experience (e.g., how much tax they pay), but also on their perception of whether the procedures that produced the outcomes are fair (e.g., they judge fairness based on what taxes others pay and the services others receive for their payments)—an idea known as "procedural fairness." [See 23, 50.] [For procedural fairness, see 46.]

the design and acceptance of changes in how much taxes residents pay and how they pay them.

How Does Local Government Affect Investment and Location Decisions?

It is difficult to measure whether local government has effects on individuals' and companies' decisions. However, anecdotal accounts suggest that fragmentation of local government creates a *hassle factor*. In particular, this may have important consequences for economic development in Allegheny County. For example, fragmented local government can create inconsistencies in policies that affect development.[7] Policies on tax rates, building codes, and permitting requirements can vary and sometimes conflict across municipalities. Fragmentation may also create an environment in which a region does not speak with one voice to prospective employers considering growing within or relocating their business to that region. Effects of the hassle factor can be seen in stories of recent commercial developments in Allegheny County. For example, the Homestead Waterfront Development was sited across three municipalities, which created the need to negotiate a tax-sharing plan to avoid preferential site selection based on taxes or building codes within this Brownfield development project. Although the negotiated plan is viewed as a success, this negotiation would not have been necessary were the county less fragmented [e.g., 16].

Other development reports suggest that fragmentation can pit municipalities against one another to attract commercial development. On one hand, this can produce a competitive environment within which businesses can operate. On the other hand, these negotiations may create transaction costs that reduce the region's overall attractiveness or merely end in a redistribution of resources within the county, rather than increasing the overall level of development in the county.

Although intangible, the hassle factor created by fragmented local government may be an important determinant of the success of economic development efforts. The few illustrations above echo a reality that every region struggles with, whether characterized by rapid or slow growth and multiple municipalities, cities, or counties [25, 4]. Local economic health is shaped by the regional economy at a regional scale. Whenever public accountability is missing at the regional level, local governments have every incentive to establish and maintain policies that benefit them locally, even at the expense of the region as a

---

[7] [For a review of the literature, see 62.]

whole. Local decisionmaking about land use and taxing provides the means to create policies that protect local interests, such as excluding housing that might burden social services, or excluding public infrastructure for waste treatment or highways that are needed in the region but not locally.

Encouraging regional involvement requires active management. For example, in its consolidation, Indianapolis created an economic development corporation to provide technical and logistical support to businesses relocating to the downtown area, and the region's elite were recruited to work with government to revitalize the central city [7, 18, 69, 83]. Throughout the process, the nonprofit sector was an active participant, responsible for one dollar out of every ten invested. More than half of the funds invested were from the private sector. In the end, for every dollar the City of Indianapolis invested, almost six additional dollars were invested [69].

A review of case histories of consolidation shows that regions often improve economically following consolidation [18, 31, 67, 69,83]. The qualification to this remark, of course, is that it is not now possible to say *ceteris paribus* whether this is a result of consolidation or other factors. There is mixed evidence about whether consolidation enhances economic development; one study [25] suggested that the form of government, per se, has *no* impact on economic development.

Anecdotes alone cannot assess the significance of this factor. However, systematic interviews with community leaders and business leaders from companies that either chose to locate in Allegheny County or thoughtfully considered investments in the county while ultimately going elsewhere can illuminate whether and, if so, how fragmentation of local government in Allegheny County affects development efforts.

4. Models of County and Regional Governance

Across the United States, communities have experimented with the structure of local government. As a result, there are many models to consider for cooperation, coordination, and consolidation of government. Each of these models enables communities to capture different benefits associated with the three components of governance discussed above: service provision, taxation, and decisionmaking.

Walker [6, 56, 81] grouped models of intergovernmental cooperation according to the perceived degree of political difficulty in initiating and managing them. Under Walker's framework, summarized in Tables 4.1 and 4.2, alternatives are more difficult if they require structural modifications to local government or transfers of authority between government entities.

Table 4.1 presents several models of coordination and cooperation that are considered "relatively easy" and "moderately difficult" to undertake. Relatively easy alternatives involve regional approaches to urban-type service delivery based on formal or informal agreements. "Moderately difficult" approaches include coordination of special districts or reformed urban counties (described as counties that provide urban-type services). Municipalities in Allegheny County already use several of the arrangements listed in the table, including, for example, private contracting, councils of governments, and regional special authorities (e.g., the regional asset district tax).

Intergovernmental arrangements that are "relatively easy" tend to focus on improving the delivery of services for one or more local governments. These actions are most closely aligned with the first two components of governance—the cost and quality of service provision and the level and fairness of tax payments. The benefits from these intergovernmental activities are relatively straightforward to assess through careful benchmarking, including comparing service costs and quality pre- and post-implementation, intra-regionally, and against other similar regions.

The arrangements identified as "moderately difficult" to establish include the third component of governance—decisionmaking—and place a greater emphasis on changes in the revenue structure compared with "relatively easy" forms of governance actions. The reasons for pursuing one of these more difficult types of governance structures may differ as well. Easier forms of governance changes may take advantage of economies of scale (e.g., joint purchasing of road salt) or improving service (combining snow removal capabilities). More difficult types of agreements tend to expand a tax base to address service deficiencies (e.g., in water or sewer treatment), to finance regional assets (e.g., cultural, sporting, or transportation facilities), to offset regional inequities (e.g., improving protective services in underserved areas), or to rationalize economic development (e.g., providing regional incentives to attract or retain businesses). Measuring the benefits from these types of actions is more complex than easier types of agreements. As above, comparisons of the costs and quality of services are needed pre- and post-implementation, and inter- and intra-regionally. In addition, it is important to compare the outcomes against the intended goals for the governance change, and to identify and redress unintended consequences.

Table 4.1
Types of Intergovernmental Cooperation, Coordination, and Consolidation by the Degree of Political Difficulty

Relatively Easy	Moderately Difficult
Informal cooperation	Local special districts
Inter-local service agreements	Transfer of functions
Joint powers agreements	Annexation
Extraterritorial powers	Regional special districts and authorities
Regional councils of governments	Metropolitan multipurpose districts
Federally encouraged single purpose districts	Reformed urban county
State planning and development districts	
Contracting with private vendors	

SOURCE: Walker, 1987 [81].

Table 4.2 presents three types of intergovernmental structures that are viewed as "very difficult" to initiate and manage: one-tier consolidation, two-tier restructuring, and three-tier reform [81]. The forms of governance presented in the table differ from those in Table 4.1 because they result in a new unit (or many units) of government.

Table 4.2
Types of Intergovernmental Governance That Are Considered Politically "Very Difficult" to Institute and Manage

One-Tier Consolidation: City-County and Area-Wide Consolidation	
Examples	Comments
Baton Rouge, LA (1949)	About 20 examples since World War II
Nashville, TN (1962)	All services and functions under one
Jacksonville, FL (1968)	governmental unit
Indianapolis, IN (1970)	Difficult to get past voters
Lexington, KY (1972)	

Two-Tier Restructuring: Federal Structures	
Examples	Comments
Miami-Dade County (1957)	"Urban-county" model
Louisville-Jefferson County (2003)	Area-wide functions separate from local
	Allows for economies of scale and local
	control

Three-Tier Reform: Metropolitan-Wide Structures	
Examples	Comments
Minneapolis-St. Paul (1967)	Only 2 examples exist
Portland, OR (1979)	No additional level of government
	Coordinated planning and infrastructure
	development

SOURCES: Walker, 1987 [81], Mitchell-Weaver, Miller, and Deal, 2000 [56].

One-Tier Consolidation

One-tier consolidation efforts result in a single government that provides all municipal services in a region, such as public schools, fire and police protection, planning and zoning, water and sewer services. Adopting this form of governance typically involves state legislative authorization plus passage of a local referendum. The results from regions that have attempted one-tier consolidation are mixed. It has generally proved difficult to achieve a consolidation to one tier. The regions that have managed to do so experienced multiple failures in earlier attempts or had long histories of cooperation agreements on which to build. Interestingly, after consolidation, the level of satisfaction and comfort grows with the new form of government. Some examples of one-tier governance include Nashville, Tennessee; Lexington, Kentucky; and Indianapolis, Indiana [56].

Nashville successfully overcame serious financial problems[8] through consolidation with Davidson County in 1962. This success is partly attributable to diversified revenue sources, including new local sales taxes, vehicle taxes, and a geographically larger property tax base [36, 83]. In addition, tax rates went down, in part, because the merged police force yielded economic savings and improved delivery of services. All consequences of consolidation were not positive. A prominent drawback cited is weakened minority representation because of the concentration of minorities within the city core. This problem was cited in other regions with diverse populations and a strong minority presence in a city [83].

In Kentucky, the inability to provide adequate police and fire services across jurisdictions in a growing metropolis led to the merger of all services in Lexington with Fayette County in 1972 [83]. The net effect on efficiency is unclear, however, since the decrease in property taxes may have been offset by increases in countywide payroll taxes and the introduction of user fees for several services.

Indianapolis merged with Marion County in 1969 in part to try to rationalize the overlap and duplication in government units and to revitalize the city and the image of the region [69, 83]. The region reported an increase in federal funding after consolidation, stemming from a larger urban population, improved economic development activity, and employment growth. However, the merger only partially consolidated the various tax bases, which meant the burdens for financing redevelopment efforts were not equally distributed. In addition, despite being described as a model for a single government, some services are still delivered by lower levels of government, leading to inequities in service delivery that are currently being addressed.

Two-Tier Restructuring

The two-tier form of restructuring governance separates regionwide functions from local ones, allowing for greater control over more closely held values and amenities at the local level (e.g., schools). Regional functions might include any systemwide service, such as highways, public transportation, sewer and water services, and waste disposal. This form of governance is seen as a compromise to the one-tier form by linking higher-level services without dissolving lower-level government control. However, the choice of which services are delivered

----
[8] Nashville reported infrastructure deficiencies, a declining tax base (urban flight), large numbers of tax-exempt businesses, and a small per-capita share of state and county taxes.

regionally or locally in practice is idiosyncratic and driven, at least in part, by constituent demands. Two prominent examples of two-tier restructuring include Miami/Dade County and Louisville/Jefferson County.

Miami and Dade County adopted a federalized form in 1957, driven by the fiscal insolvency of Miami, inadequate services, and political corruption [36, 83]. County services include transportation, airport, sewer and water, judicial courts, and the redistribution of tax revenues to jurisdictions. Municipalities provide local services, including police and fire protection. A study conducted in the 1970s concluded that taxes had increased after the merger and total net expenditures increased. Overall, consolidation remains popular with residents, although there continue to be heated debates and disagreements about the details and about extending services (e.g., sewer extension policy) [83].

The results from the recent example of two-tier governance of Louisville with Jefferson County (2003) will be closely watched. The impetus for the merging of regional services included the need to rationalize economic development planning for the county, the city's need for revenues, and the need for improvements in the delivery of public services [72, 80]. The region has participated in tax sharing and combined services since 1986, which is credited with helping to begin the area's recovery from its manufacturing decline. Accordingly, the move to formalize the management structure for a dozen city-county agencies may not have been as large a step as other regions might face.

Three-Tier Reform

Three-tier reform combines characteristics of the one- and two-tier forms of governance. A regional council provides decisionmaking and policy oversight primarily in economic development and land-use planning and in some regionwide services and functions. Unlike either of the first two forms, it does not create a new level of government. The two key examples are Minneapolis-St. Paul and Portland, Oregon. Minneapolis-St. Paul Metropolitan Council, which is appointed by the governor, was established in 1967 to coordinate planning and development [56]. Over time, the council merged with the functions of the transit authorities and the water control commission. The council oversees the regional bus system and wastewater treatment services. It provides planning, decisionmaking, and policy oversight for regional growth, affordable housing, regional parks, and other regional services (aviation, transportation, open space, water quality, and water management). There is regionwide revenue sharing to even out fiscal resources available to local governments, and there is regionwide provision of some services [55].

Portland, Oregon, adopted a three-tier structure in 1979, building on a long history of regional cooperation among special service districts and councils of governments [56]. The specific goal was to control sprawl. As such, the elected council plays a central role in transportation and land-use planning policy. The council also received decisionmaking authority for regional service functions, including solid waste disposal (1980); the stadium, coliseum, and performing arts infrastructure (1990); and the county parks system (1994) [1].

In Conclusion

The various forms of government, from cooperative agreements to one-tier consolidation, provide avenues for improving governance. But there is no "best" model that emerges from the literature on governance structure; each approach has benefits and pitfalls, and every region has its own specific challenges. Allegheny County municipalities, including the City of Pittsburgh, already use many of the relatively easier models presented in Table 4.1, and, because of recent budgetary problems for the county and city, there have been suggestions to consider some of the more difficult approaches listed in Table 4.2.

Agreement for intra-municipal sharing of services is easier when there is an existing basis of trust from earlier agreements and becomes more difficult as more players enter the game, leading to the need for more formal arrangements. Strong differences in preferences for service cost or quality among municipalities lead to disagreements in how to contract for or share services and make even relatively easy modes of governance difficult to initiate or manage. It is not surprising that consolidation efforts are politically very difficult, because, in order to find savings, service delivery tends to evolve toward the lowest common denominator, leaving many unsatisfied stakeholders for those services that do not exhibit economies of scale.

The choice of governance model(s) depends on the issues on the table, stakeholder preferences, and desired outcomes. The driver for change tends to be an imbalance between what customers pay for a service or function (usually in the form of taxes) and what they receive or expect to receive. Thus, the primary function of implementing a different governance model is to restore the balance between tax payments and a desired level of service. Other less tangible costs and benefits that may stem from various consolidation models may be just as important. They include, for example, the loss of power experienced by some as a result of restructuring and the opportunity to recast one's city as a metropolitan area with a larger population and improved statistics for median income, employment, educational achievement, and crime.

5. Toward a Model of Governance for Allegheny County

Current politics and fiscal pressures in the City of Pittsburgh and Allegheny County have pushed the issues of government fragmentation and consolidation into the headlines. The challenge facing the region is to assess whether a new vision for local governance can help address some of the challenges the region faces. A new vision would not build a government based solely on historical legacy or lessons from other regions. Rather, it would define a structure that provides efficient services, balances resources equitably, and positions the region to compete in the global market. In short, a new vision for governance is one that might retain much of what is good about small government, yet strives to capture the efficiencies that can be realized through cooperation and consolidation.

The analysis and literature reviews presented above provide insights into the links between the structure and quality of local government. Potential effects of fragmentation include those on government services, the level and perceived fairness of tax structures, and the alignment of public- and private-sector decisionmaking with regional goals.

Services, Taxes, and Decisionmaking

The effectiveness of local government services must be measured in terms of both cost and quality. Some services—particularly those that require large capital outlays like street maintenance or fire protection—provide the potential for smaller locales to realize economy-of-scale savings through consolidation. Other services, like parks and recreation or libraries, may not hold the same potential for large savings because there may not be major economy-of-scale benefits and/or because they are more driven by resident preferences for the quality of the service provided. Analysis of government expenditures for specific services in Allegheny County reveals wide variability, suggesting possible opportunities for municipalities to capture savings through cooperation or coordination. However, additional information, including the quality of service provided and resources utilized,[9] is needed to understand the extent to which these opportunities actually exist.

Lexington, Kentucky, and Indianapolis, Indiana, which have completed government consolidation, provide little if any evidence that consolidated governance leads to a lower total tax burden. Restructured governance can produce tax structures that balance inequities across a region. However, as in the case of Indianapolis, regional taxation policies need to be carefully designed to achieve a balance between the cost and benefits of government services perceived to be fair.

Finally, in areas where local governance is highly fragmented, anecdotal evidence discussed above suggests that government incentives lead to decisions that result in local gains that are made at the expense of regional advances [4, 56, 61]. These incentives exist because there is not a countervailing force to encourage decisionmaking that would provide benefits to the wider area. Other regions, such as consolidated Indianapolis, have benefited from adopting a regional decisionmaking perspective that promotes common goals for economic development and planning. However, the link between regional governance and economic growth is not universal, and associated gains of regionalism are not automatic. Allegheny County's existing fragmented government structure provides significant challenges for leaders when considering options for improving local governance.

Implications for Governance in Allegheny County

This report provides lessons that can inform discussions of local governance and government structure in Allegheny County. However, this research does not identify a suggested model of governance because the literature reviewed suggests local variations and preferences can strongly influence the success or failure of the different models of local governance. Successful attempts to improve governance in Allegheny County will be difficult unless there is a consensus on why a change is required and unless the process is supported by informed decisionmaking.

Currently in the region, discussions of the costs and benefits of alternatives for local governance are strongly influenced by perceptions of public safety responsiveness, translation of corporate best-practices to government, unfair

---

[9] Resource utilization can be measured using metrics of labor effort, capital equipment utilization, and fiscal expenditures. Thus, budget summaries do not provide a complete picture of resource utilization.

taxation, and uncontrolled and unwanted—or, to some, much welcomed though unrealized—commercial and residential development. If the region is to make progress on improving local governance, two conditions are necessary to enable meaningful discussions and informed decisions about policy alternatives.

First, the discussions must be based on a solid understanding of the current state of governance in Allegheny County. This baseline can inform how services are provided today (i.e., public, contracted, or privatized services), which functions are largely consolidated and which are highly fragmented, how much citizens of the county pay in taxes for services, and the quality of the service delivered. Much of this information, particularly that on service quality, is not currently available.

Performance measurement of municipal services serves several ends. Measurement can help improve performance by identifying areas of opportunity to develop or expand the quality of services or cut expenses. It strengthens accountability by providing transparency in service costs and quality to both government and customers. It can stimulate productivity and creativity as municipalities seek ways to improve their effectiveness. Finally, it can help Allegheny County identify opportunities for improved efficiency of local governance and assess the outcomes of policy alternatives that have been adopted. In essence, performance assessment allows leaders to understand where the county stands, to meaningfully discuss how the county should change, and to assess whether, and in what way, alternative policies could make a difference.

Second, leaders from municipalities across the county must want to engage in substantive discussions about local governance and potential cooperation or consolidation. If municipalities do not perceive benefits for themselves, they will not be active partners in any discussions. There are many reasons why municipalities in Allegheny County might participate. These municipalities are increasingly interdependent, as people commute across municipal borders to work, creating interregional economic flows. Desirable housing, a strong urban core, an effective transportation system, and open spaces are all important attributes of economically growing regions, and these attributes can be fostered only through cooperation among municipalities. The business environment faced by private-sector decisionmakers is shaped by the aggregate policies of municipalities across the county, and that environment can be improved only through cooperation. These issues provide examples of focus areas that could form the foundation for countywide discussions of governmental cooperation and consolidation. However, meaningful discussion across Allegheny County will be difficult unless points such as these can be supported with strong evidence.

Agreeing on any new model for local governance requires (1) knowing what the attributes of a region currently are, (2) agreeing on what it wants to become, and (3) having an informed understanding of the likely benefits and costs of various routes for getting there. Each step is challenging. The examples presented in this preliminary report provide an overview of the important characteristics of local government and examples from other regions of achievements gained through restructuring. More definitive information, along the lines discussed above, can provide a foundation for more in-depth discussions and possibly an incentive to move forward. If potential benefits are apparent, this effort can help to define a unified vision and set of goals for governance and economic development in Allegheny County.

Appendix

Analysis of Government Expenditures on Public Services in Allegheny County

Analysis of per-capita expenditures on government services provides simple insights into the performance of local governance. These data can reveal trends in the level of fragmentation that exists in service provision, the potential for realizable cost savings by coordination of government services, and the importance of measuring the level and quality of government services. As an example, Figure A.1 presents per-capita municipal expenditures on streets and roads in Allegheny County.

As shown in the figure, most of the 130 municipalities in Allegheny County maintain independent budgets for street servicing and repair, which includes snow removal, deicing, and street cleaning. The dots on the graphic are the per-capita municipal expenditures calculated from individual municipal budgets. Almost all of the 130 municipalities in the county have a budget for these services. For presentation purposes, the City of Pittsburgh (population 369,789) is presented as a line rather than a point. For comparison purposes, lines are also provided for the per-capita costs for Louisville (population 256,231) and Indianapolis (population 791,926).

The data in Figure A.1 document two important facts. First, per-capita street and road expenditures in most municipalities in Allegheny County (represented by the dots), including the City of Pittsburgh, are comparable to or lower than those for Louisville and Indianapolis. This suggests that spending across most of the county is aligned with other regions with similar demographic and economic profiles.

Second, variability in per-capita expenditures—typically toward higher expenditures—is much greater for smaller municipalities (i.e., those with populations lower than 10,000). For example, Pine Township (population 4,048), the Borough of Thornburg (population 461), and the City of Clairton (population 9,656) spend five to six times more per resident than the City of Pittsburgh.[10]

---

[10] In addition to measures of quality, it would be important to calibrate the expenditure figures with information on utilization, e.g., lane-miles per capita or number of snow days.

Figure A.1
Per-Capita Expenditures on Streets and Roads Services in 2001
for Municipalities in Allegheny County

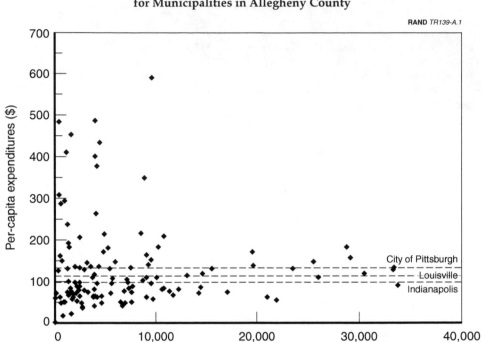

NOTES: Points on the graph represent municipalities other than the City of Pittsburgh. The city, Louisville, and Indianapolis are shown with lines on the graph for comparison of per-capita costs. Variability in per-capita costs increases for municipalities with fewer than 10,000 residents.

An examination of per-capita expenditures for parks and recreation (Figure A.2) highlights the extent to which local decisions on the level and quality of services influence government budgets. Data in Figure A.2 do not make a clear case that economies of scale exist for parks and recreation expenditures. At the same time, there remains significant variability in per-capita expenditures for these services across municipalities.

Figure A.2
Per-Capita Expenditures on Parks and Recreation in 2001
for Municipalities in Allegheny County

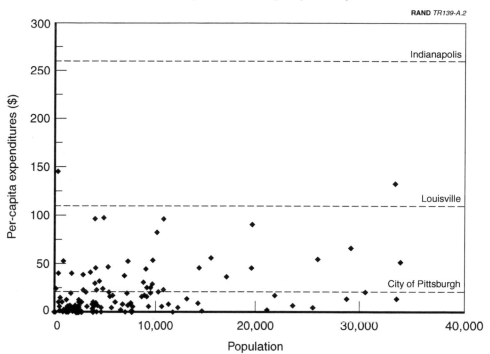

NOTES: Points on the graph represent municipalities other than the City of Pittsburgh. The city, Louisville, and Indianapolis are shown with lines on the graph for comparison of per-capita costs. Variation in expenditures of municipalities in Allegheny County is independent of population, perhaps because expenditures are more directed by resident preferences.

In contrast, data suggest that there are natural economies of scale for provision of street and road services. However, these data do not provide enough information to identify the sources of variability in street and road services nor do they provide enough information on the absence of variability in park services. Information on quality and level of services is required because the variation across municipalities may be significant. Without better data, however, there is considerable uncertainty about what "high" costs mean. High costs for small municipalities may reflect an inability to capture economies of scale, inadequate management, or a local decision to provide more than the typical level or quality of service. Likewise, lower expenditures for smaller communities may reflect efficient provision, good management, or a local decision to provide fewer street and road services. For example, Mount Lebanon (population 33,362) spends about four times what the City of Pittsburgh spends on public parks per resident, although dozens of smaller municipalities spend little to nothing on public parks.

Furthermore, both Louisville and Indianapolis spend significantly more on parks and recreation than most municipalities in Allegheny County. Once again, data on quality of these services are required to assess whether a municipality is paying too much for what it is managing.

The case studies described above shed some light on the performance of local government in Allegheny County. They also set the foundation to motivate discussions among municipalities in the county about what benefits might be available from increased cooperation on service provision. Analysis that is more thorough could provide guidance about where improvements in local government might be possible and what alternative approaches may prove beneficial. An extended analysis would more completely address the range of services provided by governments in the county. It would also address issues identified above (i.e., quality of services, revenue generation, and decisionmaking) to support cost analysis like that presented here.

References

1. Abbott, Carl, and Margery Post Abbot, "Historical Development of the Metropolitan Service District," prepared for the Metro Home Rule Charter Commission, Portland, OR, 1991. Online at www.metro-region.org/article.cfm?ArticleID=2937 (as of April 2004).

2. Ammons, David N., ed., *Accountability for Performance: Measurement and Monitoring in Local Government*, Philadelphia, PA: International City/County Management Association, 1995.

3. Baldassare, Mark, Joshua Hassol, William Hoffman, and Abby Kanarek, "Possible Planning Roles for Regional Government," *Journal of the American Planning Association*, Winter 1996.

4. Barbour, Elisa, and Michael Teitz, *A Framework for Collaborative Regional Decision-Making*, San Francisco: Public Policy Institute of California, 2001.

5. Becker, Fred W., and Milan J. Dluhy, "Consolidation Versus Fragmentation of Government Services: Evidence from Metropolitan Miami," in Fred W. Becker and Milan J. Dluhy, eds., *Solving Urban Problems in Urban Areas Characterized by Fragmentation and Divisiveness*, Stamford, CT: JAI Press, 1998.

6. Bish, Robert L., *Regional District Review—1999: Issues and Interjurisdictional Comparisons*, Victoria, British Columbia, Canada: Local Government Institute, University of Victoria, 2003. Online at http://web.uvic.ca/lgi/reports/rd/rdtoc.htm (as of April 2004).

7. Blomquist, William, "Fiscal, Service, and Political Impacts of Indianapolis-Marion County's UniGov," *Publius*, Vol. 25, No. 4, 1995.

8. Bollman, Nick, *The New California Dream: Regional Solutions for 21st Century Challenges*, Sacramento, CA: California Institute for County Government, 2002.

9. Brunori, David, "Metropolitan Taxation in the 21st Century," *National Tax Journal*, Vol. 51, No. 3, 1998, pp. 541–551.

10. Calabrese, Stephen, "Local Government Fiscal Structure and Metropolitan Consolidation," *Brookings-Wharton Papers on Financial Services*, 2002.

11. Campbell, Richard W., and Sally Coleman Selden, "Does City-County Consolidation Save Money? The Unification of Athens-Clarke County Suggests It Might," *Public Policy Research Series*, University of Georgia, Vol. 1, No. 2, 2000.

12. Carruthers, John I., and Gudmundur F. Ulfarsson, "Fragmentation and Sprawl: Evidence from Interregional Analysis," *Growth and Change*, Vol. 33, No. 3, 2002, p. 312.

13. Citizens' Viewpoint, *2001 Survey: Local Government Cooperation and Consolidation*, Penn State University, 2001.

14. Clingermayer, James C., and Richard C. Feiock, *Institutional Constraints and Policy Choice*, Albany: SUNY Press, 2001.

15. Condrey, Stephen E., "Organizational and Personnel Impacts of Local Government Consolidation: Athens-Clarke County, Georgia," *Journal of Urban Affairs*, Vol. 16, 1994, pp. 371–383.

16. "Creeping Change: Consolidation Gains Support, Even in Allegheny County," *Pittsburgh Post-Gazette*, Editorial, October 13, 2003. Online at www.post-gazette.com/pg/03286/230370.stm (as of April 2004).

17. DeAngelis, James P., "Forum: If Not Quantity, Then Quality," *Pittsburgh Post-Gazette*, April 14, 2001. Online at www.post-gazette.com/forum/20010415eddeang7.asp (as of April 2004).

18. DeBoer, Larry, and Jeffery P. Mann, "City-County Consolidation for Indiana: An Outline of the Issues," *Purdue University Cooperative Extension Service Circular*, October 1990.

19. Deller, Steven C., David G. Hinds, and Donald L. Hinman, *Local Public Services in Wisconsin: Alternatives for Municipalities with a Focus on Privatization*, Madison: Dept. of Agricultural and Applied Economics, University of Wisconsin-Madison, 2001.

20. Dilger, Robert Jay, "Privatization of Municipal Services in America's Largest Cities," *Public Administration Review*, Vol. 57, No. 1, 1997.

21. Durning, Dan, and Patricia Dautel Nobbie, "Post-Transition Employee Perspectives of City-County Unification: The Case of Athens-Clarke County," *Public Administration Quarterly*, Vol. 24, No. 2, 2000, pp. 140–168.

22. Durning, Dan, "The Effects of City-County Government Consolidation: The Perspectives of United Government Employees in Athens-Clarke County, Georgia," *Public Administration Quarterly*, Vol. 19, 1995, pp. 272–298.

23. Fehr, E., and K. M. Schmidt, "A Theory of Fairness, Competition and Cooperation," *Quarterly Journal of Economics*, Vol. 114, No. 3, 1999, pp. 817–868.

24. Feiock, Richard C., and Fred Seamon, "Political Participation and City/County Consolidation: Jacksonville-Duval County," *International Journal of Public Administration*, Fall 1995.

25. Feiock, Richard C., and Jared B. Carr, "A Reassessment of City/County Consolidation: Economic Development Impacts," *State and Local Government Review*, Vol. 23, No. 3, Fall 1997, pp. 166–171.

26. Fitzpatrick, Dan, "PG Benchmarks: Just the Facts on Taxes" *Pittsburgh Post-Gazette*, November 24, 2002. Online at www.post-gazette.com/benchmarks/20021124taxes3.asp (as of April 2004).

27. Giannatasio, Nicholas A., "Worms and Coffee: Municipal Consolidation in the South," *Public Administration Quarterly*, Vol. 25, No. 1, 2001, pp. 79–100.

28. Gonzalez, Oscar, "Previous Consolidation Efforts in the Global Metropolitan Region of El Paso, Texas," *Public Administration Quarterly*, Vol. 24, No. 2, 2000, pp. 246–274.

29. Harrison, Russell, *The Costs and Benefits of Local Government Consolidation*, Camden: Rutgers School of Law, 1998.

30. Hatry, Harry P., *Performance Measurement: Getting Results*, Washington, DC: Urban Institute, 1999.

31. Hatry, Harry P., Louis H. Blair, Donald M. Fisk, John M. Greiner, John R. Hall, Jr., and Phillip S. Shaenman, *How Effective Are Your Community Services?* Washington, DC: Urban Institute, 1992.

32. Heikens, Norm, "Indianapolis Sparkles, Study Says," *Indianapolis Business Journal*, Vol. 19, No. 21, 1998.

33. Heikens, Norm, "UniGov Under a Microscope," *Indianapolis Business Journal*, Vol. 19, No. 37, 1998.

34. Honadle, Beth Walter, and Patricia Love, "Choices for Change: A Guide to Local Government Co-operation and Restructuring in Minnesota," *Minnesota Cities*, Vol. 81, 1996, pp. 9–14.

35. Hoyt, William H., "Differences in Tax Bases and Tax Effort Across Kentucky Counties," Working Paper, Lexington, KY: Center for Business and Economic Research (CBER), University of Kentucky, 2003.

36. Johnson, Linda S., and Richard C. Feiock, "Revolutionary Change in Local Governance: Revisiting the Rosenbaumm and Kammerer Theory of Successful City County Consolidation," *The Journal of Political Science*, Vol. 27, 1999, pp. 1–29.

37. Johnson, Robin A., and Norman Walzer, *Local Government Innovation: Issues and Trends in Privatization and Managed Competition*, Westport: Quorum, 2000.

38. Joint Center for Sustainable Communities, "Growing Together: City/County Smart Growth Profiles," Washington, DC: Joint Center for Sustainable Communities, 1999.

39. Keil, Roger, "Governance Restructuring in Los Angeles and Toronto: Amalgamation or Secession?" *International Journal of Urban and Regional Research*, Vol. 24, No. 4, 2000, pp. 758–781.

40. Kelsey, Timothy W., "What Are the Important Issues Facing Pennsylvania?" *Farm Economics*, Vol. 6, 2001.

41. Koven, Steven G., "Consolidation of Rural Service Delivery," *Public Productivity and Management Review*, Vol. 15, 1992, pp. 315–328.

42. Langley, Michael, "The Private Sector: 'Brain Drain' No Surprise in Our City of Colleges," *Pittsburgh Post-Gazette*, November 11, 2003. Online at www.post-gazette.com/pg/03315/238105.stm (as of April 2004).

43. Lavery, Kevin, "How Are Services Provided?" in *Smart Contracting for Local Government Services*, Westport: Praeger, 1999, pp. 26–38.

44. Legislative Council Service, Survey of Privatization Initiatives in New Mexico State Government, House Joint Memorial 21, Forty-fourth Legislature, second special session, Santa Fe, NM: Legislative Council Service, 2001.

45. Leland, Suzanne, and Kurt Thurmaier, "Metropolitan Consolidation Success: Returning to the Roots of Local Government Reform," *Public Administration Quarterly*, Vol. 24, No. 2, 2000, pp. 202–222.

46. Lind, E. A., and T. R. Tyler, *The Social Psychology of Procedural Justice*, New York: Plenum Press, 1988.

47. Liner, Blaine E., Pat Dusenbury, and Elisa Vinson, *State Approaches to Governing-for-Results and Accountability*, Washington, DC: Urban Institute, 2000.

48. Liner, Blaine E., Harry P. Hatry, Elisa Vinson, Ryan Allen, Pat Dusenbury, Scott Bryant, and Ron Snell, *Making Results-Based Government Work*, Washington, DC: Urban Institute, 2001.

49. "Local Governments?" *Farm Economics*, No. 6, 2001.

50. Loewenstein, G. F. T. L., and M. H. Bazerman, "Social Utility and Decision Making in Interpersonal Contexts," *Journal of Personality and Social Psychology*, Vol. 57, No. 3, 1989, pp. 426–441.

51. Lyons, William, "Saying 'No' One More Time: The Rejection of Consolidated Government in Knox County, Tennessee," *State and Local Government Review*, Vol. 30, Spring 1998, pp. 92–105.

52. Mattoon, Richard H., "Can Alternative Forms of Governance Help Metropolitan Areas?" *Economic Perspectives*, Vol. 19, No. 6, 1995, pp. 20–32.

53. McKay, Jim, "Jobless Rate Steady Despite Sagging Factory Sector," *Pittsburgh Post-Gazette*, October 28, 2003. Online at www.post-gazette.com/pg/03301/234649.stm (as of April 2004).

54. Mead, Timothy D., "Governing Charlotte-Mecklenburg," *State and Local Government Review*, Vol. 32, No. 3, Fall 2000, pp. 192–197.

55. Minneapolis-St. Paul Metropolitan Council, "About Us." Online at www.metrocouncil.org/about/about.htm (as of April 2004).

56. Mitchell-Weaver, Clyde, David Miller, and Ronald Deal, Jr., "Multilevel Governance and Metropolitan Regionalism in the USA," *Urban Studies*, Vol. 37, No. 5/6, May 2000, pp. 851–876.

57. Morley, Elaine, Scott Bryant, and Harry P. Hatry, *Comparative Performance Measurement,* Washington, DC: Urban Institute Press, 2001.

58. Noack, David, "Crossing the Boundaries," *American City and County*, Vol. 108, No. 10, 1993.

59. Orfield, Myron, and Bruce Katz, *American Metropolitics: The New Suburban Reality,* Washington, DC: Brookings Institution Press, 2002.

60. Orfield, Myron, *Metropolitics: A Regional Agenda for Community and Stability,* Washington, DC: Brookings Institution Press, 1997.

61. O'Toole, James, "Pittsburgh Residents, Suburbanites Differ Sharply on City/County Merger," *Pittsburgh Post-Gazette*, October 7, 2003. Online at www.post-gazette.com/localnews/20031007papoll1007p1.asp (as of April 2004).

62. Paytas, Jerry, "Does Governance Matter? The Dynamics of Metropolitan Governance and Competitiveness," Working Paper, Pittsburgh, PA: Carnegie Mellon University, December 2001.

63. Pennsylvania Economy League, "State and Local Tax Burdens," 2003. Online at www.issuespa.net/scorecards/366/ (as of April 2004).

64. Post, Stephanie, "Local Government Cooperation: The Relationship Between Metropolitan Area Government Geography and Service Provision," Annual Meeting of American Political Science Association, Boston, Massachusetts, October 2002. Online at www.fsu.edu/~localgov/papers/archive/PostStephanie.pdf (as of April 2004).

65. Prefontaine, Lise, Line Ricard, Helene Sicotte, Danielle Turcotte, and Sharon Dawes, *New Models of Collaboration for Public Service Delivery,* Quebec City, Quebec, Canada: CEFRIO, 2000.

66. Rabidoux, Greg R., "Are American Taxpayers Receiving the Municipal Services They Have Paid for?" Dissertation, Milwaukee: University of Wisconsin, 2002.

67. *Regional Comparisons Reveal Strengths and Challenges for Central Indiana,* Indianapolis: Center for Urban Policy and the Environment, Indiana University, School of Public and Environmental Affairs, Indiana University-Purdue University, September 2003.

68. Ritchie, Ingrid, and Sheila Suess Kennedy, *To Market, To Market: Reinventing Indianapolis*, Lanham: University Press of America, 2001.

69. Rosentraub, Mark S., "City-County Consolidation and the Rebuilding of Image: The Fiscal Lessons from Indianapolis's UniGov Program," *State and Local Government Review*, Vol. 32, No. 3, 2000, pp. 180–191.

70. Rubin, Charles, "Forum: The False Hope of Regionalism," *Pittsburgh Post-Gazette*, September 14, 2003. Online at www.post-gazette.com/pg/03257/225526.stm (as of April 2004).

71. Sanger, Mary Bryna, *When the Private Sector Competes*, Washington, DC: Brookings Institution Press, 2001.

72. Savitch, H. V., and Ronald K. Vogel, "Metropolitan Consolidation Versus Metropolitan Governance in Louisville," *State and Local Government Review*, Vol. 32, No. 3, 2000, pp. 198–212.

73. Segedy, James A., and Thomas S. Lyons, "Planning the Indianapolis Region: Urban Resurgence, de Facto Regionalism and UniGov," *Planning Practice and Research*, Vol. 16, No. 3/4, 2001, pp. 293–305.

74. *Sustainable Pittsburgh, Southwestern Pennsylvania Citizens' Vision for Smart Growth: Strengthening Communities and Regional Economy*, Pittsburgh: Sustainable Pittsburgh, 2002.

75. Swanson, Bert E., "Quandaries of Pragmatic Reform: A Reassessment of the Jacksonville Experience," *State and Local Government Review*, Vol. 32, No. 3, Fall 2000, pp. 227–238.

76. "Symposium: Is City-County Consolidation Good Policy?" *Public Administration Quarterly*, Vol. 24, No. 2, 2000, pp. 133–245.

77. Teitz, Michael, J. Fred Silva, and Elisa Barbour, *Elements of a Framework for Collaborative Regional Decision-Making in California*, San Francisco, CA: Public Policy Institute of California, 2001.

78. Temple, David G., *Merger Politics: Local Government Consolidation in Tidewater*, Charlottesville, VA: University Press of Virginia, 1972.

79. University Committee of Merced, *Impact of the University of California Campus at Merced on the Regional Economy*, Merced: University of California, 1997.

80. Vogel, Ronald K., "Metropolitan Planning Organizations and the New Regionalism: The Case of Louisville," *Publius*, Vol. 32, No. 1, 2002, pp. 107–129.

81. Walker, D. B., "Snow White and The 17 Dwarfs: From Metro Cooperation to Governance," *National Civic Review*, Vol. 76, 1987, pp. 14–28.

82. Wheeler, Stephen M., "The New Regionalism: Key Characteristics of an Emerging Movement," *Journal of the American Planning Association*, Summer 2002.

83. White, Sammis, *Cooperation Not Consolidation: The Answer for Milwaukee Governance*, Thiensville: Wisconsin Policy Research Institute, 2002.